PICTURE FACTS

COMBAT AIRCRAFT

PICTURE FACTS

COMBAT AIRCRAFT

C. J. Norman

Franklin Watts

London   New York   Sydney   Toronto

Published by:

Franklin Watts
96 Leonard Street
London EC2A 4RH

Franklin Watts Australia
14 Mars Road
Lane Cove
NSW 2066

ISBN: Paperback edition   0 7496 0473 5
        Hardback edition   0 86313 351 7

Copyright © 1986 Franklin Watts

Paperback edition 1990

Hardback edition published
in the Picture Library series.

Printed in Singapore

Designed by
Barrett & Willard

Photographs by
Boeing Military Airplane Company
British Aerospace
Lockheed Aircraft Corporation
Ministry of Defence (UK)
Naval Photographic Center, Washington DC
Panavia
Shorts Brothers
US Air Force
S. Willard
N. S. Barrett Collection

Illustration by
Stuart Willard and Janos Marffy

Technical Consultant
Bernard Fitzsimons

Series Editor
N. S. Barrett

Contents

Introduction

Combat aircraft have many uses in modern warfare. Bombers strike at enemy targets. Fighter planes provide defence against strike aircraft and intercept enemy fighter planes.

Other roles, or duties, for warplanes include transporting troops and equipment, and observing enemy positions and movements.

△ A Viggen fighter-bomber of the Swedish Air Force. The Viggen has an advanced design. Its main wings are at the back in place of a tailplane, with smaller wings in front.

Today's combat aircraft cost billions of pounds to design and build. They contain complex electronic systems, including computers that control every movement.

Aircraft can operate at almost any altitude. Some fly nearly to the edge of space. Other aircraft skim across the earth just above ground level.

△ A Fighting Falcon, or F-16, of the US Air Force. As well as performing its duties as a fighter, the F-16 may be used as a strike aircraft, as can be seen from the clusters of bombs carried under its wings.

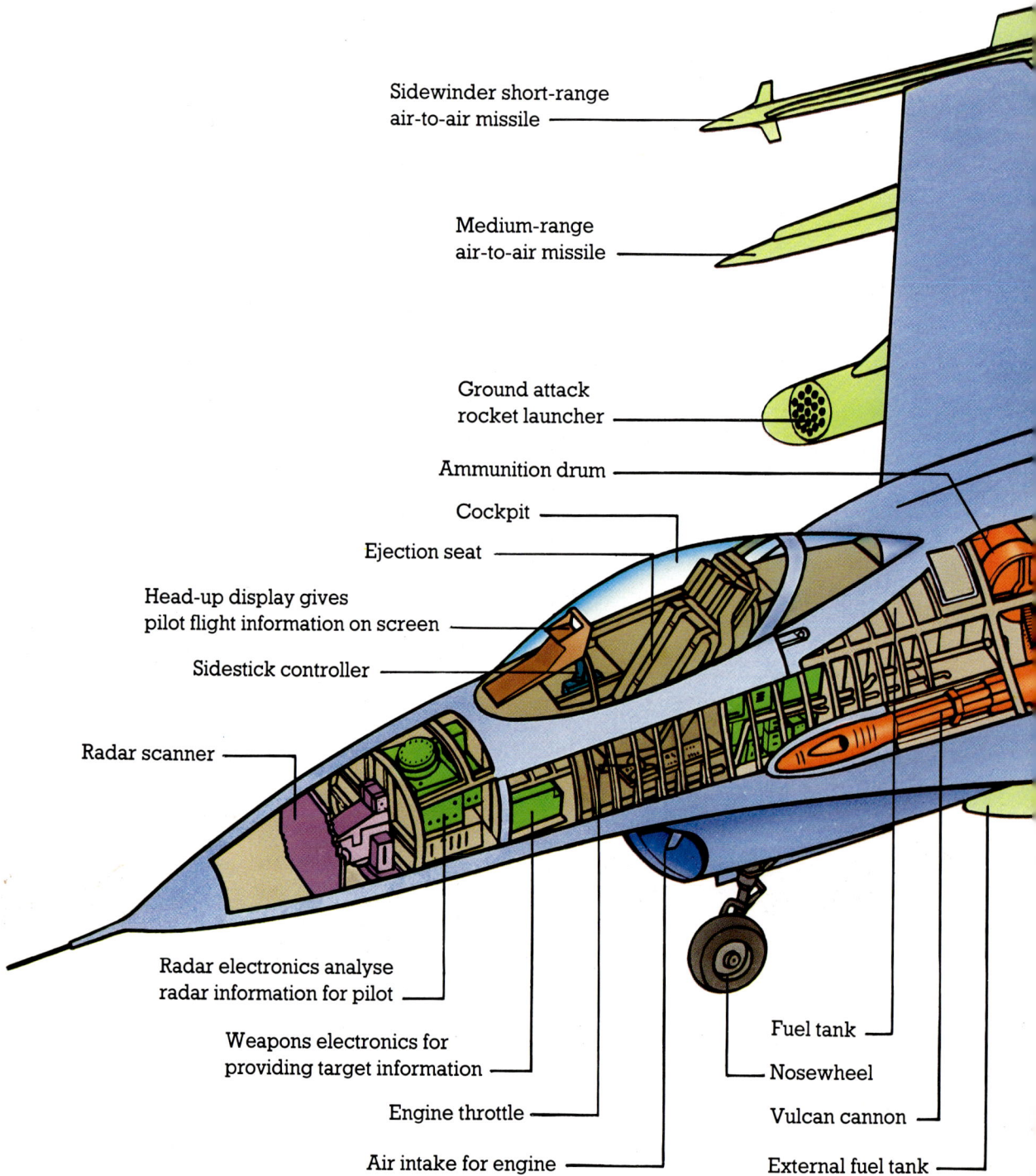

The warplane

Sidewinder short-range
air-to-air missile

Medium-range
air-to-air missile

Ground attack
rocket launcher

Ammunition drum

Cockpit

Ejection seat

Head-up display gives
pilot flight information on screen

Sidestick controller

Radar scanner

Radar electronics analyse
radar information for pilot

Weapons electronics for
providing target information

Engine throttle

Air intake for engine

Fuel tank

Nosewheel

Vulcan cannon

External fuel tank

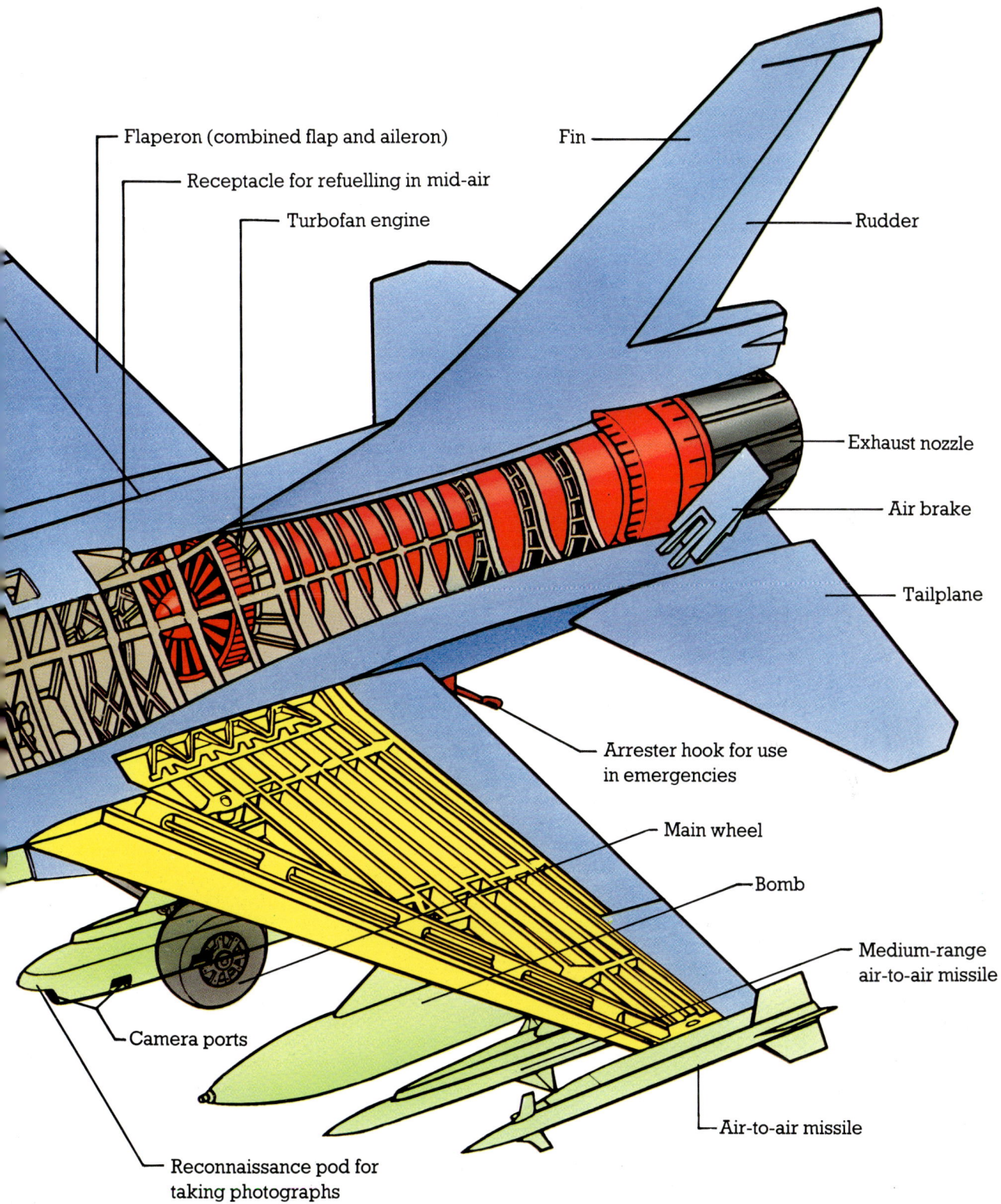

Flaperon (combined flap and aileron)

Fin

Receptacle for refuelling in mid-air

Turbofan engine

Rudder

Exhaust nozzle

Air brake

Tailplane

Arrester hook for use in emergencies

Main wheel

Bomb

Medium-range air-to-air missile

Camera ports

Air-to-air missile

Reconnaissance pod for taking photographs

Kinds of warplanes

The latest warplanes can serve as either bombers or fighters. They are called multi-role aircraft.

For bombing duties, an aircraft is armed with bombs and air-to-surface missiles. Fighters are equipped with cannon and anti-aircraft missiles.

Special planes are used for such duties as reconnaissance, carrying troops and refuelling in mid-air.

▷ The Sea Harrier is a multi-purpose aircraft. This one is carrying anti-ship missiles. But its chief role is as a fighter plane providing air defence for its own carrier and the rest of the fleet.

▽ A Tomcat and a Corsair (right) are refuelled in mid-air by a tanker, a Boeing 707 airliner converted for military duties.

Fighter planes

There are two main kinds of fighter aircraft. One type, such as the Fighting Falcon or the Hornet, is for close-combat "dogfights" with enemy aircraft. Close-combat planes can be manoeuvred sharply at high speed.

The other type, such as the Tornado or the Tomcat, has an "interceptor" role. It lies in wait for the enemy and then attacks with long-distance missiles.

▽ A Tomcat fighter (left) is launched from the flight deck of an aircraft carrier. An Eagle (right) comes in to land. The flap behind the cockpit is an air-brake.

▷ "Foxbats" are very fast Soviet interceptor fighters. They climb very rapidly and can fire missiles when out of sight of the enemy.

▽ Hornet fighters lined up on the deck of an aircraft carrier. Hornets, or F-18s, are used for "dogfight" combat. They can be manoeuvred sharply at high speeds.

▷ The Tornado is a tandem, or two-seater, interceptor fighter. It has "swing wings", like some other supersonic warplanes. Swing wing planes operate more efficiently at low speeds with their wings in the forward position, as in the picture. For supersonic speeds, they fly with their wings swept back towards the tail.

The two large, white cigar-shaped objects attached to the wings are tanks for carrying extra fuel. Four Skyflash long-range missiles are attached under the body. One of the plane's two Sidewinder short-range missiles can be seen next to a fuel tank.

△ The B-1, seen refuelling behind a tanker, is the latest US strategic bomber.

▷ Inside the cockpit of a B-52. The screens show the height of the terrain ahead, so that the planes can be flown close to the ground to avoid enemy radar.

△ A Tornado strike
aircraft. This is shorter
than the interceptor
version. It can fly at
supersonic speed close
to the ground and at
twice the speed of
sound at higher levels.

◁ A view from the
rear seat of a low-
flying Jaguar. It is
designed to operate
from roads if airfields
are put out of action.

▷ A jump-jet aircraft is easily hidden because it does not need a runway for landing or taking off.

▽ An AV-8B, one of the latest jump-jet strike aircraft. It is a new version of the Harrier, built jointly by Britain and the United States with the most advanced materials to improve its capabilities.

Smaller strike aircraft such as the Tornado can fly low into enemy territory. They attack such targets as supply columns, enemy airfields and radar stations.

Other strike aircraft are used at the battlefront. Planes such as the Jaguar, Harrier and Thunderbolt attack ground and sea targets with guns, bombs and missiles.

▽ The A-10 Thunderbolt was designed as a "tank buster". It has heavy armour plating so the pilot and engines are specially protected from ground fire. It has a very powerful cannon and is armed with Maverick air-to-ground missiles.

Weapons

Fighters carry cannon and anti-aircraft missiles. Strike aircraft may be equipped with bombs, air-to-surface missiles, torpedoes and mines. Many weapons are aimed, fired and guided automatically. Strike aircraft also have guns and missiles for their own protection.

▽ A Tornado on display with a range of weapons. These include Sidewinders, the missiles with the arrow-shaped heads, and a variety of bombs. At the back are parachute-retarded bombs. These are dropped from low levels.

Most aircraft are equipped with
two 20 or 30 mm (0.8 or 1.2 in)
cannon. Some have one rotary
cannon which fires its rounds
faster.

The missiles carried by a plane
depend on its role. Different
missiles are used for such purposes
as air defence and ground attack,
or against ships and submarines.

Aircraft carry many types and
sizes of bombs. Some are guided
to their targets by lasers.

△ A cruise missile
being launched from
an A-6 Intruder. Cruise
missiles fly low to
avoid detection by
radar. They have a
complex computer
system to enable them
to fly a long-distance
route with great
accuracy. They can
carry nuclear
warheads.

△ Anti-aircraft missiles are fired from sea- and land-based launchers as well as from other planes. An aircraft can be brought down even by a hand-held weapon, such as the Javelin shown in the picture.

◁ The Sidewinder, a heat seeking missile, homes in on the exhaust of a plane's engines.

Reconnaissance planes

Reconnaissance missions include observing enemy movements on land and sea and in the air. Special planes are equipped for this.

Aircraft such as the Blackbird fly high and fast. They photograph military areas. Other reconnaissance planes have powerful radar to detect incoming enemy aircraft or missiles.

▽ **The Blackbird is a high-flying reconnaissance plane. It photographs areas such as military bases and searches for the location of nuclear missiles.**

Transport planes

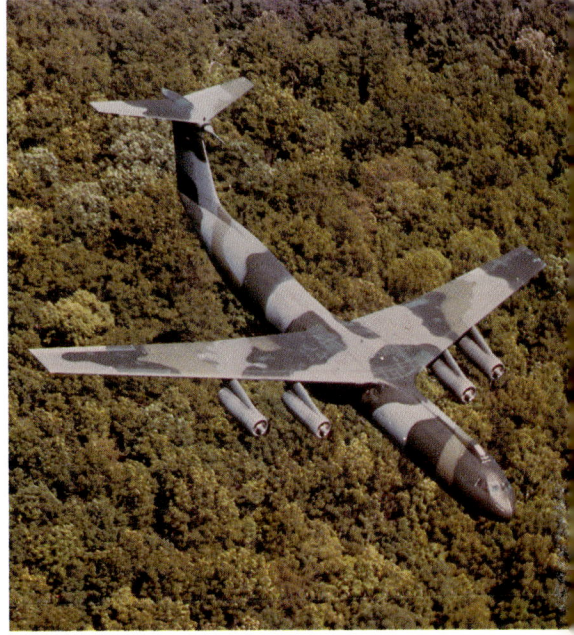

Special planes carry troops, supplies and military equipment. They have large bodies, usually with a wide opening at the back or front so that fighting vehicles such as tanks or helicopters can enter.

Transport planes either land to unload their troops and cargo or drop them into the battle zone by parachute.

There are also tankers which carry aviation fuel for mid-air refuelling.

△ The Sherpa (left) is a light transport plane for carrying troops or spare parts for military vehicles.

The Starlifter (right) is a large jet troop carrier. It can also be used as an ambulance plane or for carrying freight.

The story of combat aircraft

The first warplanes

The first warplanes, in the early 1900s, were used for reconnaissance. Most of the early aircraft were called biplanes because they had two sets of wings. They were light craft, powered by small petrol engines. But some reached speeds of 120 km/h (75 mph) and could fly as high as 3,000 m (10,000 ft).

World War I aircraft

The use of aircraft for military purposes developed in World War I (1914–18). It started when the pilots of reconnaissance planes began to fire pistols at each other. Guns were then fitted in the cockpit. Pilots dropped bombs over the side. Soon, larger planes were designed specifically for dropping bombs. Fighter planes were built to intercept the bombers. They were equipped with machine guns and were easier to manoeuvre. As many as fifty planes often took part in a single dogfight.

Unusual aircraft

Among the combat aircraft of World War I were airships and seaplanes. The Germans used Zeppelin airships for reconnaissance and bombing. The navies of the warring nations used seaplanes. These were aircraft with floats that enabled them to take off from land or water. Flying boats were seaplanes with a boat hull.

△ A World War I artist's impression of a typical dogfight between British and German fighters.

△ A Scapa, a reconnaissance flying boat of the 1930s. On a flying boat, the fuselage is like the hull of a boat and keeps the plane afloat on the water. The two floats keep it stable.

World War II planes

In the 1930s, biplanes were replaced by monoplanes, which have one pair of wings. With better design, stronger materials and more powerful piston engines, aircraft reached speeds of 500 km/h (300 mph).

Great advances in the design and development of warplanes were made in World War II (1939–45). The Spitfire, a British fighter, could fly at 565 km/h (350 mph). The German Messerschmitt Me-262 was the first jet warplane. Hundreds of thousands of planes were built during the war. The US alone built nearly 300,000.

△ A photograph taken in 1951 comparing a giant bomber of the time, a B-36, with a tiny Curtiss-type biplane built in 1912.

Later progress

After the war, more great

△ A photograph taken in 1960 to commemorate the Battle of Britain (1940) shows wartime and post-war fighters. From the left: Hurricane, Spitfire and Meteor (all wartime), Hunter and Javelin (both early 1950s), and Lightning (late 1950s).

advances were made in aircraft design. Swept-back wings and other changes of shape helped planes fly faster – more than twice the speed of sound. Jump-jets were introduced. Today's combat aircraft often have a double role of fighter and bomber.

△ A Jaguar strike aircraft of today. This plane is being used as a model for systems being tested for future aircraft.

Facts and records

Combat balloons

The first combat aircraft were balloons. People first flew in balloons in the 1700s. The balloons were filled with gas or hot air. As long ago as 1794, the French Army sent up soldiers to observe enemy movements and positions.

△ The Neptune, a French reconnaissance balloon of 1870. It was used to observe the movements of the Prussians, who had laid siege to Paris. The balloon was effective because it was out of reach of the enemy's guns.

Fastest and highest

The Blackbird reconnaissance plane of the US Air Force is the fastest combat aircraft and the highest flier. A Blackbird has reached a speed of 3,529 km/h (2,193 mph). This is more than Mach 3, or 3 times the speed of sound. Blackbirds can fly at more than 25,000 m (82,000 feet). A Soviet "Foxbat" has flown higher, but only for short periods.

The deadly Swordfish

The Royal Navy used Swordfish biplanes on its carriers during World War II. It was a Swordfish that torpedoed and damaged the German battleship *Bismark*, enabling British battleships to catch and sink her. The *Bismark* was the most powerful ship in the world, but it could not shoot down the Swordfish because its guns could not track such a slow-flying aircraft.

△ Many old aircraft, such as the Swordfish, still fly at air displays.

Glossary

Dogfight
Air combat between fighters.

Interceptor
A fighter plane that defends against attacking aircraft with long distance missiles.

Jump-jet
Another term for a STOVL aircraft.

Mach number
A measure of the speed of planes in relation to the speed of sound. Mach 1 is the speed of sound, Mach 2 twice the speed of sound.

Parachute-retarded bomb
A bomb dropped from a low flying aircraft. Its fall is slowed by a parachute to allow the plane to fly to safety before the bomb explodes.

Radar
A method, using special radio waves, for detecting objects such as aircraft or for locating a craft's own position. Radar may also be used for guiding missiles.

Reconnaissance
A mission to observe the enemy or to check whether enemy forces are present.

Rotary cannon
A gun with several revolving barrels, so that more shells are fired per minute.

STOVL
A plane that can operate from a small space, such as a clearing on the ground or the deck of a small ship. The letters stand for Short Take-Off and Vertical Landing.

Strategic bomber
An aircraft used to strike at vital targets outside the battle zone, such as military bases or arms factories.

Supersonic
Flying faster than the speed of sound. At sea level, the speed of sound is 1,225 km/h (761 mph), but decreases as a plane climbs higher and the air gets thinner.

Swing wings
Wings that can be moved backwards and forwards in flight. The different positions give the aircraft the best possible wing shapes at various speeds.

Index